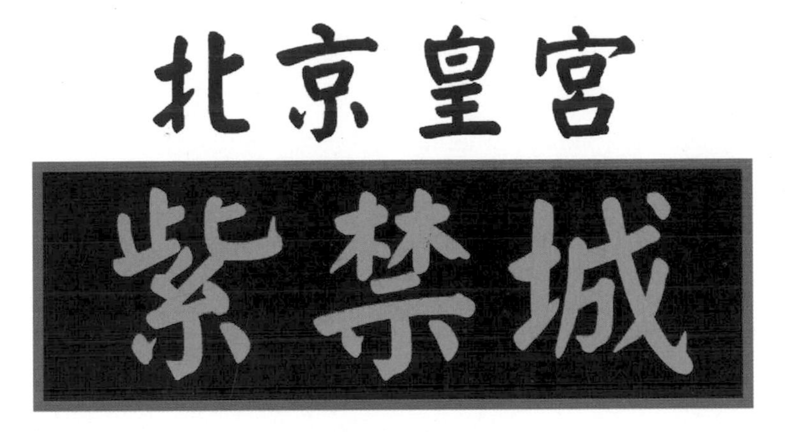

The Forbidden City
–Former Imperial Palace

人民中国出版社
PEOPLE'S CHINA PUBLISHING HOUSE

图书在版编目（CIP）数据

北京皇宫·紫禁城/宇辰编著. —北京：人民中国出版社，2000. 6

ISBN 7-80065-693-4

Ⅰ. 北… Ⅱ. 宇… Ⅲ. 故宫－简介 Ⅳ. k928. 74

中国版本图书馆CIP数据核字（2000）第62303号

First editon 2000

ISBN 7 - 80065 - 693 - 4/J. 112

Published by the People's China
Publishing House, Beijng, China
No. 3 Chegong road Beijing, 100044
Printed in the People's Republic of China

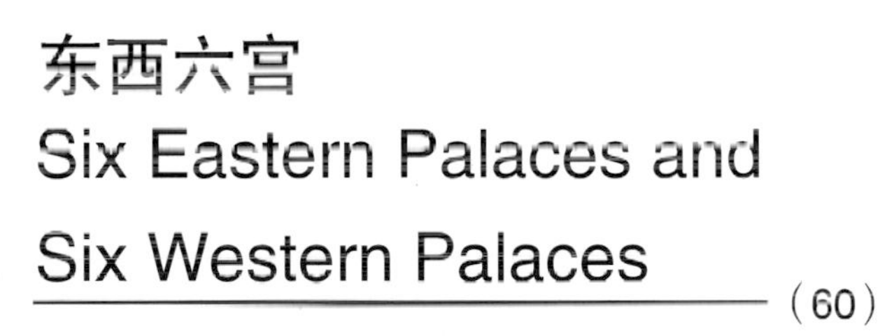

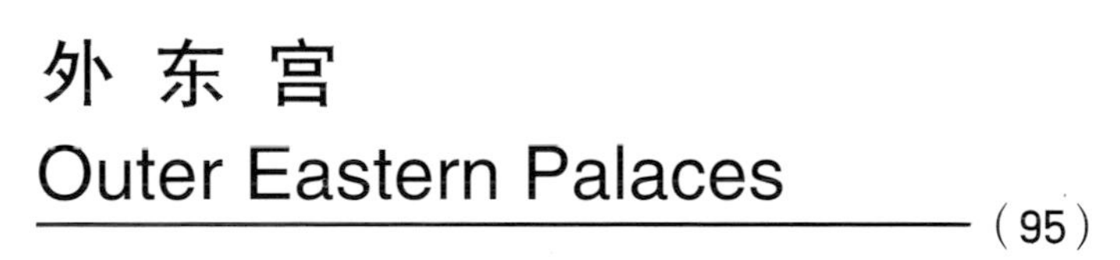

前　言

紫禁城是中国明（1368－1644）、清（1644－1911）两朝皇宫。“紫”是紫微星的简称，民间传说此星为天帝星座，以星喻帝；“禁”意为皇帝居住的地方，又有禁地、禁区的意思。1925年成立故宫博物院，紫禁城俗称故宫。

故宫始建于明永乐15年（1417），3年后建成，1421年明代正式从南京迁都北京。至今故宫有近600年历史。

故宫座落于北京城南北中轴线，它南起永定门，北至钟鼓楼，全长8公里，皇家禁苑部分约占1/3。整个建筑以中轴线为中心展开，天安门为其序幕，外朝三大殿形成高潮，景山为其终曲。整体建筑主从分明，跌岩起伏，前呼后应，左右对称，由此形成了宫廷区乃至整个北京城的宏伟气魄和井然秩序。仅在宫廷区范围内，共有殿堂馆舍号称9999间半（现存8000余间），建筑面积约15万平方米，占地72万平方米。为了建造这座巨大的“城中之城”，明王朝倾全国人力物力，征调能工巧匠10万余名，民夫逾百万，所用建筑材料采自全国各地，真可谓“量中华之物力，给人间之仙阙”，堪为中国古代宫殿建筑之最。

故宫平面为长方形，其四周由高10米、长约3.4公里的宫墙围括，墙四隅各设造型别致的角楼一座。宫墙四面分别建有宫门，南为午门，北为神武门，东为东华门，西为西华门。墙外环绕护城河，河宽52米，长3.8公里，河水清幽，终年不断。

故宫作为中国古代建筑的代表作，其布局分外朝、内廷两部分。外朝以太和、中和、保和三大殿为主体，左右衔连文华、武英两殿。三大殿以北为内廷，内廷又分中、东、西三路，中为乾清宫、交泰殿、坤宁宫，其后是御花园；中路两侧为东、西六宫。东六宫向南是奉先殿、斋宫、南三所，西六宫向南为养心殿。内廷的外围东有宁寿全宫，西有慈宁、寿安诸宫。这种布局，充分体现了古礼所谓“前朝后寝”的格局。前朝为“大内正衙”，后寝即所谓“三宫六院”。

如此恢宏浩繁的建筑群，所以未给人杂乱纷繁、局促拥塞之感，主要因为突出了一条极为明显的中轴线和重点突出、简繁得体的建筑手法。建筑群以太和殿为重中之重，它巍然座落于前朝的中心位置。这里是皇家政治活动的中心，皇帝继位、大婚、朝会、殿试及命将出征均在此举行，所以它的体量最大，等级最高，充分体现了皇权第一的思想。同在中轴线上的内廷主体建筑如乾清宫、交泰殿和坤宁宫，虽然也是帝、后经常活动和处理政务的主要场所，在一定程度上实用性甚至超过外朝三大殿，但它们毕竟不是重大活动的中心，所以它们的建筑规模、体量和豪华程度明显逊于太和殿，表现出严格的“内外有别”。再以各殿飞檐的垂脊兽为例，太和殿设置10尊，乾清宫设置9尊，交泰殿设置7尊；而中轴线两侧的东西六宫各主要大殿仅设置5尊。由此不难看出，紫禁城内人与人之间复杂的等级关系，即封建社会的等级制度，在这里被明白无误的建筑形式完整地体现出来了。等级是权力的象征，也是皇权赖以维系的基础，这其中政治与礼制的内涵，被我们聪明的古代匠人以简洁明快的物质架构昭示于世人。

故宫不仅建筑精美，而且宫内各种家具、隔扇及陈设，无不精雕细琢，古色古香，使人叹为观止。除此以外，宫藏文物异常丰富，且不说1949年被国民党政府运往台湾的2927箱珍宝，现珍藏于故宫的文物珍品就达100多万件。人们无论走进殿堂、寝宫或斗室，总能观赏到奇珍异宝、古玩遗墨。为满足广大游客观赏的需要，故宫管理者在外东路专门设立了珍宝馆和钟表馆，辟出若干殿堂展示文物精品。如本书介绍的青玉云纹灯，为战国（公元前475－前221）遗物，王公专用，此灯玉质青润细腻，灯柱和上盘边沿阴刻美丽花纹，圆形台座凸雕云朵，造型生动，既实用，又可作工艺品摆放。又如元代（1271－1368）青花釉盖罐，以青花为主调，以剔花为特色，是中国瓷器的巅峰之作，堪为国宝。其他诸如印玺、法书、名画、漆器、珐琅、金银器及各种宝石制品，大部分为世所罕见的珍宝极品。人们徜徉珍宝馆，既可看到上古玉器、青铜，又可见中古名画、墨宝，可谓琳琅满目，美不胜收，真所谓“华夏之美，美在文化，文化之美，尽萃故宫”。

故宫以其完美的古代建筑艺术，丰富的文化艺术藏品和厚重的人文精神内涵，成为中国古代文明的象征。中华人民共和国成立以后，每年拨巨款对它维修和保护。现在的故宫，已成为中国最负盛名的旅游热点。

Foreword

The Forbidden City in Beijing was the imperial palace of the Ming (1368-1644) and the Qing (1644-1911) dynasties. In 1925 it was changed to the Palace Museum, also known as the former Imperial Palace.

The construction of the Imperial Palace started in the 15th year of the Yongle Reign of the Ming Dynasty (1417) and was completed three years later. In 1421, the Ming Dynasty moved its capital from Nanjing to Beijing. Now the Imperial Palace is nearly 600 years old.

The entire Imperial Palace area takes up one-third of the 8-kilometre-long central axis of the old Beijing city from the gate of Yongdingmen on the south to the Drum and Bell Towers on the north. Along the central axis, the palace building complex starts from the Gate of Heavenly Peace (Tian'anmen), centres on the Outer Court and ends at the Jingshan Hill. This harmonious assemblage of buildings displays the best characteristics of Chinese architecture -- majestic style, flawless construction and fine coordination of the whole and the parts. Within the Imperial Palace, all together there are 9,999 and half bays of palaces and halls (over 8,000 bays are now extant), in a total building space of 150,000 square metres, covering an area of 720,000 square metres. To build such a large "city within the city", the Ming-dynasty rulers used the whole country's manpower and material resources. A hundred thousand artisans and a million workmen were conscripted on the project, and building materials were gathered from all parts of the country.

The Imperial Palace, rectangular in shape, is surrounded by a 10-metre-high and 3.4-kilometre-long city wall, with an exquisitely-built Corner Tower at each of the four corners. On the four sides of the city wall are four gates: the Meridian Gate (Wumen) on the south, the Gate of Divine Prowess (Shenwumen) on the north, the East Flowery Gate (Donghuamen) on the east, and the West Flowery Gate (Xihuamen) on the west. Outside the city wall is the 52-metre-wide and 3.8-kilometre-long moat, which has water in it all the year round.

The Imperial Palace is the representative of ancient buildings in China. It is composed of the Outer Court and the Inner Court. In the Outer Court along a single axis are the three main halls: the Hall of Supreme Harmony (Taihedian), the Hall of Central Harmony (Zhonghedian), and the Hall of Preserving Harmony (Baohedian). On either side of them are two minor halls: the Hall of Literary Glory (Wenhuadian), and the Hall of Martial Spirit (Wuyingdian).

The buildings in the Inner Court are arranged along three lines. On the central line are the three main halls: the Palace of Heavenly Purity (Qianqinggong), the Hall of Union (Jiaotaidian), and the Palace of Earthly Tranquillity (Kunninggong). At the northern end of this line is the Imperial Garden. Parallel to the central line are the Six Western Palaces and the Six Eastern Palaces. To the south of the Six Eastern Palaces are the Hall of Worshipping Ancestors (Fengxiandian), the Palace of Abstinence (Zhaigong) and Nansansu; to the south of the Six Western Palaces is the Hall of Mental Cultivation (Yangxindian). On the eastern side of the three main halls is the Palace of Tranquil Longevity (Ningshougong); on the western side are the Palace of Motherly Tranquillity (Cininggong) and the Palace of Longevity and Peace (Shou'angong). Such exquisite layout fully shows the etiquette of the ancient times that "court is in the front and living quarters are at the rear". So the Imperial Palace has the throne in the front court and the "Three Palaces and Six Yards" in the back.

The huge building complex of the Imperial Palace is so well arranged that all the structures are completely free from the sense of being crowd and clumsy. This is because a distinctive central axis is used, and the predominant features of architecture are stressed in the construction. The Hall of Supreme Harmony, the centre of the emperor's activities, is the most important building located in the middle of the Outer Court. It is here that grand ceremonies, such as the accession of a new emperor to the throne, the emperor's wedding, the audiences the emperor gave to officials, imperial examination, appointment of army commanders, were held. This magnificent building fully displays the imperial authority. The buildings on the central axis in the Inner Court, such as the Palace of Heavenly Purity, the Hall of Union and the Palace of Earthly Tranquillity, are inferior to the Hall of Supreme Harmony in terms of size, quality and the degree of magnificence, although they were also the main places where the emperor and empress handled state affairs, and to a certain extent, played a bigger role in reality than the three halls in the Outer Court. It is because they were not the centre of the emperor's activities. This shows the etiquette conception that "The Outer Court is different from the Inner Court". Another example is the zoomorphic ornamental animals on the roof ridges of the buildings. The Hall of Supreme Harmony has ten such animals on each of its roof ridges, the largest number allowed. The Hall of Preserving Harmony has nine, the Hall of Central Harmony has seven, and the main halls in the Six Eastern Palaces and Six Western Palaces have only five. It manifested the supreme power of the emperor and strict hierarchy of feudal China.

Another feature of the Imperial Palace is its large number of exquisitely made furniture, partition screens, tables and chairs. They are the acme of perfection. Treasures and cultural relics in the Imperial Palace are extremely rich. In addition to the 2,927 large trunks of treasures the Kuomintang government took to Taiwan in 1949, the treasures and cultural relics now housed in the Imperial Palace amount to over one million pieces. One feels entering an art display in every building. In order to meet the needs of visitors, two special exhibitions have been set to display the treasures and timepieces. The Jade Lamp with Cloud Design introduced in this album is a fine example. The lamp was handed down from the Warring States period (475-221 B. C.). The edge and the post of the lamp are carved in intaglio with beautiful designs, and the round stand of the lamp is carved in relief with cloud design. It is a masterpiece of art with great practical and ornamental value. Another fine example is the Blue and White Glazed Porcelain Jar of the Yuan Dynasty (1271-1368). A representative of the peak period of porcelain making in China, the porcelain jar is a big treasure. Other objects like imperial seals, paintings, calligraphic works, lacquerware, enamels, gold vessels, silverware and various kinds of gems, all are rarities of the world. In the treasures exhibition hall, one is dazzled by the endless array of beautiful exhibits from the jade articles and bronzes of the remote ages to the treasured paintings and scrolls of calligraphy of the middle ages. Really, "the beautiful essence of China lies in its culture, and the beautiful essence of the culture lies in the Imperial Palace."

With its perfect architectural art, large quantity of historic relics and embodiment of rich culture, the former Imperial Palace has become the symbol of ancient Chinese civilization. Since the founding of the People's Republic in 1949, the Chinese government has allotted a huge sum of money for its maintenance and protection every year. Today, the former Imperial Palace is the hottest tourist attraction in China.

前　朝

The Outer Court

是故宫建筑物的重中之重。对旅游者来说，大体包括从天安门至保和殿一组完整的建筑群，即故宫中轴线建筑的前半部；严格意义上的前朝，应从太和门算起，以太和、中和、保和三大殿为中心，文华、武英二殿为两翼。前朝是宫廷举行典礼、朝贺、筵宴的地方，故建筑物以高大、宏阔、豪华为特征，以表现皇家宫殿的至尊至贵以及皇权统治的绝对权威。

The Outer Court is the most important part of the building complex of the Imperial Palace. It includes the complete building group from the Gate of Heavenly Peace (Tian'anmen) to the Hall of Preserving Harmony (Baohedian) -- the front part of the Imperial Palace along the central axis. To be exact, the Outer Court starts from the Gate of Supreme Harmony (Taihemen) and centres on three main halls: the Hall of Supreme Harmony (Taihedian), the Hall of Central Harmony (Zhonghedian) and the Hall of Preserving Harmony (Baohedian). On either side of the three main halls are two minor halls: the Hall of Literary Glory (Wenhuadian) and the Hall of Martial Spirit (Wuyingdian). As the place was where the emperor conducted state affairs, all the structures of the Outer Court are grand and magnificent, symbolizing the supreme power of the imperial rule.

故宫远眺 故宫位于北京城中心，南北长960米，东西宽750米，周长3420米。现称故宫博物院，正式对外开放。南北各设出入口，南系午门，北为神武门。图为从景山眺望故宫。

Bird's-eye view of the Imperial Palace Located in the centre of Beijing city, the Imperial Palace is 960 metres long from south to north and 750 metres wide from east to west and 3,420 metres in circumference. It is now called the Palace Museum open to visitors. It has two entrances: Meridian Gate (Wumen) in the south and the Gate of Divine Prowess (Shenwumen) in the north.

天安门　始建于明永乐15年（1417），称“承天门”；原为明、清两代皇城正门。历史上曾多次被雷火焚毁，1651年重修后改称“天安门”。它原为皇帝颁发诏令和重大政务活动的出入之门，建筑规制甚高，五洞城门，重楼九楹。天安门实为中国首都的象征。

Gate of Heavenly Peace (Tian'anmen) Originally built in 1417 and named Chengtianmen, it was the front gate of the Imperial Palace during the Ming and Qing dynasties. It was burnt down and rebuilt several times. After rebuilding in 1651, it was renamed Tian'anmen with five openings, double-eaved roof and nine columns, serving as a gate the emperor passed through to attend major activities. The imposing gate tower today is a symbol of the People's Republic of China.

天安门鸟瞰　天安门前原为皇城御河，河上横跨汉白玉石桥5座，桥栏上雕饰着精美的龙凤云图案。天安门城楼前是世界上最大的广场－天安门广场。

Bird's-eye view of the Gate of Heavenly Peace In front of the gate lies the Imperial River with five white marble bridges across it. On the balustrades of the bridges are carved exquisite patterns of dragon, phoenix and clouds. Before Tian'anmen Gate Tower is the world's largest square -- Tian'anmen Square.

天安门华表　天安门前后各立华表一对。中国的华表起源甚早，初为木制，为纳谏而设，后发展成路标，称华表。华表顶蹲神兽名为“犼”。天安门后华表犼头朝里，寓意皇帝不可沉缅宫廷享乐，应常出宫体恤民情，故叫“望君出”；前华表犼头向外，警示皇帝不要迷恋山水，应当回朝勤政，故叫“望君归”。

Huabiao　Before and behind the Gate of Heavenly Peace stand two pairs of carved white marble columns called "huabiao". The original huabiao, made of wood, was erected for the ruler to solicit criticisms from the common people. It eventually became a land mark and finally an ornamental object. The squatting mythical animal at the top of each column is called "hou". The ones behind the gate face toward the palace meaning that the emperor mustn't indulge in the cozy life there but must go out to know the populace and the ones in front of the gate face outward to suggest that the emperor must return in time from an inspection tour to attend to state affairs.

宫墙　为特制青砖垒砌，长3428米，高约10米，顶设垛口，以供巡逻将士瞭望；宫墙四隅各建角楼一座。

Palace wall　Built with specially made gray bricks, the palace wall is 3,428 metres long and about 10 metres high. At the top of the wall are crenels. At each of the four corners stands a uniquely constructed tower.

金水河　中国古代因防御需要，但凡城池，均设护城河；皇宫为绝对禁区，故设御河，又称外金水河（午门内还有内金水河）。此河宽52米，水深约2米，全长3.8公里。

Golden Water River　All cities had moats in ancient China. The imperial palace was a forbidden area, and its moat was called the imperial river, also known as the Outer Golden Water River (the one inside the Meridian Gate is called the Inner Golden Water River). The river is 52 metres wide, about 2 metres deep and 3.8 kilometres long.

►

午门　系禁城门户，守卫森严。此门居中向阳，位当子午，故名午门。城台上建崇楼5座，俗称“五凤楼”。门为5洞，中门供帝、后出入，叫“御路”，王公大臣走左右门，掖门平时不开，唯殿试时，文武进士分单双号分进左右掖门。

Meridian Gate (Wumen)　The largest gate of the Palace, it stands on the central axis of Beijing city and, as it is surmounted by five pavilions, it is also known as "The Five-Phoenix Tower". The gate has five openings. The central one was used exclusively by the emperor. Court officials passed through the two gates near the central one. The two sidegates were opened only to let in successful candidates of imperial examinations.

午门晨曦
Morning at the Meridian Gate

铜狮　座落于太和门前左右，是故宫诸铜狮中体量最大的两座。中国古人造狮，有较完备的传统体制，凡雄狮大多右足踏绣球，象征权力和一统天下，雌狮左足抚幼狮，象征子嗣昌盛。故宫诸狮，概莫能外。

Bronze Lions　The two bronze lions placed on either side of the Gate of Supreme Harmony are the heaviest of all bronze lions in the Palace. According to the traditional system of lion making in ancient China, the male lion has a carved ball under its right paw, symbolizing the imperial power, and the female lion has a baby under its left paw, symbolizing fertility of the royal family. All the lions in the Palace were made in this tradition.

太和门　中国的所谓“门”并非专指带门框的两扇门，凡设在正屋或正殿前的必通过的建筑物统称“门”或“门楼”，即使寻常人家亦不例外。太和门为故宫等级最高的门，重檐庑殿顶，上覆黄琉璃瓦，金碧辉煌，系外朝三大殿的正门。

Gate of Supreme Harmony (Taihemen) The gate here does not mean the door with a doorframe and two door planks. It refers to all buildings at the entrance to the main hall or palace. It holds true even for all ordinary households. The Gate of Supreme Harmony, the main entrance to the Outer Court, is the tallest of all gates in the Palace, a magnificent building with a double-eaved, yellow-tiled roof.

►

太和广场　为太和殿前空阔场地，占地3万多平方米，正中为巨石铺成的“御路”，其两侧为磨砖对缝的“海墁”砖地。每逢大典，御道两侧设置铜制品级山，文东武西，诸大臣依官阶跪拜于品级山旁。

Square of the Hall of Supreme Harmony The open ground in front of the Hall of Supreme Harmony covers more than 30,000 square metres. The central "Imperial Road" is paved with large stone slabs and the rest with bricks. On major occasions, bronze markers were placed along the sides of the "Imperial Road" and court officials knelt in the order of ranks.

◄

弘义阁 太和广场西侧清代设庑共33间，中间为弘义阁，重楼9间，高25米，为银库；广场东侧建筑与西雷同，中间重檐建筑为体仁阁，为绸缎库。所有库房均属清内务府管辖。

Pavilion of Enlarging Right Conducts (Hongyige) Standing on the western side of the Square of the Hall of Supreme Harmony, the pavilion is 25 metres high and has nine bays and a roof of double eaves. It served as a treasury of the Qing Court to store silver. The buildings on the eastern side of the Square are similar to the western side, and the double-eaved pavilion in the middle is Tiren Pavilion, which was a storehouse to keep silks and satins. All storehouses were controlled by the Ministry of Home Affairs in the Qing Dynasty.

外朝三大殿 是故宫最主要的建筑群，从右至左分别为太和、中和、保和殿，这里是皇帝举行大典、召见群臣和行使权力的主要场所。

The three main halls of the Outer Court The three halls, Taihe, Zhonghe and Baohe, are the most important building complex in the Palace. They were the place where the emperor held grand ceremonies, granted officials audiences and wielded power.

丹陛　外朝三大殿均座落于"工"字形台基上，台基为3层，统称丹陛，总高8.13米，每层台阶均横卧地袱，绕以汉白玉石护拦，护栏立望柱1458根，柱头精雕云龙云凤图案。地袱下设排水沟，沟口安置龙头1142个，每逢雨天，台上水从龙口排出，可谓"小雨如注，大雨如瀑"，千龙喷水，蔚为壮观。

Imperial Terrace (Danbi)　The three main halls of the Palace stand on a vast three-tiered marble terrace which is 8.13 metres high and edged with 1,458 white marble balusters carved with patterns of dragons and phoenixes. At the base of these balustrades are 1,142 gargoyles in the shape of dragon head which make a spectacle during a downpour.

铜鹤　鹤为青春长寿之鸟，传言可活万年，皇帝乞活万岁，江山代代相传，以鹤喻寿，故置于殿侧。

Bronze Crane　The crane is a bird symbolizing youthfulness and longevity. It is said that the bird can live for ten thousand years. The ones placed in front of the Hall of Supreme Harmony were to wish the emperor a long life.

铜龟 陈设于太和殿丹陛左右侧，铜龟、铜鹤均有延年益寿之意。它们铸造精工，其背有铜活盖，腹与口相通，凡遇大典，内燃檀香、沉香及松柏枝，口中香烟袅袅，环绕宫宇，大大增加了神秘和庄严气象。

Bronze Tortoise Bronze tortoises are placed on the right and left sides of the three-tiered marble terrace of the Hall of Supreme Harmony, because bronze tortoises and bronze cranes are symbols of longevity. The exquisitely cast bronze tortoise has a moveable lid, and its hollow belly is interlinked with its mouth. In the old days during a grand ceremony, sandalwood, agalloch eaglewood and cypress branches were burnt inside the hollow belly of the tortoises, which poured forth coiling smokes around the hall so as to create a mysterious and solemn atmosphere.

鎏金铜缸　清乾隆年间（1736－1795）铸造，分别置于太和殿、保和殿和乾清门前左右两侧，每缸重约2吨，鎏金100两。八国联军侵入北京时，用刺刀刮走黄金，至今刀痕尚存。宫中铜缸主要用于贮水防火。每遇大典则用黄布遮罩，显得气象庄严肃穆。故宫共有铁、铜缸308口，1944年侵华日军劫走铜缸66口，至今未归。

Gilded Bronze Vat Cast in the Qianlong Reign of the Qing Dynasty (1736-1795), these gilded bronze vats are placed on either side of the Hall of Supreme Harmony, the Hall of Preserving Harmony and the Gate of Heavenly Purity. They weigh two tons each, and each is gilded with one hundred taels of fine gold. When the Eight-Power Allied Forces invaded Beijing, the soldiers scraped the gold off the vats with their bayonets. The scrapes are still clearly visible today. These huge vats were used to store water for fire prevention. During grand ceremonies they were wrapped up with yellow cloth to add solemnity to the atmosphere. All together there were 308 iron or bronze vats in the Palace, but the Japanese invaders looted 66 of them away in 1944.

太和殿　俗称金銮殿，建于1420年。大殿面阔11间，进深5间，重檐庑殿顶，通高37.44米，总面积2377平方米。此殿是中国现存最大的木构殿。明、清两代皇帝即位、大婚、朝会以及元旦赐宴、命将出征和殿试进士等，均在此举行。

Hall of Supreme Harmony (Taihedian) Commonly known as the Hall of Gold Throne, the magnificent structure was built in 1420. It is 11 bays wide, 5 bays deep, 37.44 metres high, covering a floor space of 2,377 square metres. It is the largest wood structure extant in China. During the Ming and Qing dynasties, grand ceremonies such as the emperor's enthronement and wedding, proclamation of imperial edicts, New Year celebration, appointment of commander-in-chief of expedition troops, and receiving successful candidates of imperial examination were held here.

◀
太和殿内景 殿内陈设如当年帝、后临朝状。6根蟠龙金漆柱中央为高约2米的地平台，上设明代金漆雕龙宝座，座后为髹金屏风。殿内金碧辉煌，庄严华贵。明清两代曾有24个皇帝在此登极，宣布“即位诏书”，接受群臣朝贺。

Inside the Hall of Supreme Harmony The interior of the hall is preserved as in ancient times. The six huge gilded columns have dragons coiling around them. On the raised platform is the gilded imperial throne placed on a dais two metres high. Behind the throne is a carved screen. It looks extremely resplendent and magnificent. During the Ming and Qing dynastics, 24 emperors were enthroned here.

宝座 为故宫诸宝座之魁。宝座上半部为圈椅靠背，背上金龙缠绕，下部为座基，宝座后为7扇金龙屏风。1915年袁世凯称帝时宝座被般走，下落不明，1959年在故宫库房找到，经修复放置原位，一展当年风采。

Throne The painted golden throne with a splendid screen behind it stands on a two-metre high dais in the centre of the Hall of Supreme Harmony. Its back and the lower part are covered with coiled dragons. Warlord Yuan Shikai moved it from the hall in 1915 when he proclaimed himself emperor. In 1959 it was found in the storehouse of the Palace and restored to its original place.

大柱　太和殿内有东西向大柱12根，南北6行，总计72根。其中居中6根通体贴金，光彩照人。

Gilded Columns The Hall of Supreme Harmony has 72 huge columns with 12 in a range from east to west and 6 in a range from north to south. The six columns in the centre are entirely gilded.

中和殿　位于太和殿后，为深广各5间的方形殿，其顶为单檐四角攒尖顶。凡太和殿举行大典时，皇帝先在此接受各部大员礼拜，后去太和殿御殿。

Hall of Central Harmony (Zhonghedian) The square hall with a pyramidic roof stands behind the Hall of Supreme Harmony. The emperor would take a rest and meet high officials before he went to attend grand ceremonies in the Hall of Supreme Harmony.

中和殿内景 内设地平床，上置宝座、屏风，床下殿面有金鼎和熏炉等。殿左右存放皇帝在宫中使用的交通工具-肩舆。

Inside the Hall of Central Harmony The throne is placed on a dais in front of a screen. When the emperor came to the hall, incense would be burnt in the burners at the foot of the dais. Sedan chairs which were used to carry the emperor inside the imperial palace were put on either side of the hall.

肩舆 俗称轿子，此轿饰黑漆金云龙纹，8人抬，为清乾隆年间制造，距今约250年。

Sedan Chair Imperial sedan chair was carried by eight people. This sedan chair painted in dark lacquer with the patterns of dragons and clouds was built in the Qianlong Reign of the Qing Dynasty. It is about 250 years old now.

保和殿　“保和”即保世间关系协调之意，大殿为重檐9脊歇山顶。明代册立皇后时，太子、大臣在此上表朝贺；清代公主下嫁，皇帝在此宴请驸马，王公大臣陪宴。16世纪末以后，这里一直是科举殿试的场所。

Hall of Preserving Harmony (Baohedian) The meaning of the hall's name is to keep the world in harmony. The hall has a double-eaved roof with nine ridges. In the Ming Dynasty ceremonies were held in this hall to grant titles on the empress and the crown prince. In the Qing Dynasty the emperor gave banquet here in honour of his son-in-law when the princess got married. From the end of the 16th century onward the final session of the Civil Service Examination was held in this hall with the supervision of the emperor.

保和殿内景 内置地平台，台上为金漆宝座，无御案；宝座左右分别放置珐琅镶金宝象。中国许多朝代把象作为仪仗前导，称为仪象。清代仿历代遗制，仪仗用象；象还有象征天下太平、五谷丰登之意，故列于宫廷，俗称太平有象。

Inside the Hall of Preserving Harmony The splendid throne is on a platform at the centre of the hall. But there is no imperial desk. Two enamel elephants inlaid with gold are placed on either side of the throne. In ancient China many dynasties took the elephant as the guide of a guard of honour. The Qing Dynasty followed the example of its predecessors and used the elephant as guard of honour. The elephant is also the symbol of world peace and good harvest. So it is found in the Palace.

►

大石雕 嵌于保和殿后，系用整块艾叶青石雕刻而成，长16.57米，宽3.07米,厚1.7米,重约250吨。石雕周边浅刻蕃草纹，中刻9条蟠龙行距于流云之中；两侧浮雕海马、双狮图案。石雕选材之巨，构图之妙，雕凿之精，堪称一绝。

Huge Stone Carving Placed behind the Hall of Preserving Harmony, the large carving is made of a whole piece of stone. It is 16.57 metres long and 3.07 metres wide, weighing about 250 tons. The border of the stone is carved with the designs of plants, while in the central part are nine dragons amidst drifting clouds. This exquisite stone carving is really a wonder.

保护雕石
请勿入内

内　廷
The Inner Court

泛指乾清门以北，延至东西六宫。为方便旅游者游览参观，本书内廷仅涉及中轴线乾清门至御花园部分，其中主要介绍乾清宫、交泰殿和坤宁宫。它们是内廷最高等级的建筑群，也是帝、后频繁活动的中心，许多军国大事在这里决断，许多惊世骇俗的事件在这里发生，至今仍有许多文物保存在宫中，见物思古，能给人以无限的幽思与联想。

The Inner Court refers to the area in the north of the Gate of Heavenly Purity (Qianqingmen) including the Six Eastern Palaces and the Six Western Palaces. Here we concentrate on the buildings along the central axis from the Gate of Heavenly Purity to the Imperial Garden with emphasis on introducing the Palace of Heavenly Purity (Qianqinggong), the Hall of Union (Jiaotaidian) and the Palace of Earthly Tranquillity (Kunninggong). They are the most important building complex in the Inner Court, serving as the living quarters of the emperor and empress, where many important decisions were made and many soul-stirring events took place. Today a great number of cultural relics are preserved in these palaces, which serve as a reminder of the past.

铜狮　列于内廷乾清门前左右两侧，将内廷门户衬托得典雅富丽、豪华气派。

Gilded Bronze Lion
Bronze lions are placed on either side of the Gate of Heavenly Purity. They serve as a foil for the magnificent gate.

内廷鸟瞰 从右至左分别为乾清宫、交泰殿、坤宁宫，总称后三宫，其后为御花园。后三宫与前朝三大殿一样，座落于“工”字形台基上，共有三进九座院落。周围廊庑共设12门，从东西各门可通向众妃嫔居住的东、西六宫。这些宫殿就是民间传说的“三宫六院”，住着“粉黛三千”。实际上，明代妃嫔及宫女最多时曾达到9000余人。

Bird's-eye view of the Inner Court The Palace of Heavenly Purity, the Hall of Union and the Palace of Earthly Tranquillity are known as the Three Rear Palaces. Behind them is the Imperial Garden. Like the Outer Court, the Three Rear Palaces also stand on a three tiered marble terrace. They are in three layers and have nine yards with 12 gates around them. The gates on the eastern and western sides lead to the Six Eastern Palaces and the Six Western Palaces. Folk people call these buildings "the three palaces and six yards" where "three thousand beautiful young women" lived. In fact, the imperial concubines and imperial palace maids reached 9,000 for a time in the Ming Dynasty.

乾清门雪景 图为从乾清宫丹陛看乾清门。此门为内廷正门，面阔5间，进深3间，开3门，朱门安在后檐柱部位，使门厅宽敞而庄重。清代自康熙皇帝（1662－1722在位）起，在此“御门听政”，门厅正中设宝座、御案，百官按序分立东、西阶，分次奏事。

Gate of Heavenly Purity (Qianqingmen) The Gate of Heavenly Purity, the main entrance to the Inner Court, is five bays wide and three bays deep, with three openings. It looks magnificent and solemn. Beginning from Emperor Kangxi (reigned from 1662 to 1722), the Qing emperors sometimes gave audience to government officials at this gate.

乾清宫　建于1420年。宫为重檐庑殿顶，高24米，面阔9间，深5间，饰以沥粉点金、双龙和玺彩画，是内廷等级最高的建筑。明、清两代皇帝以此为寝宫，并在此处理朝政，皇帝驾崩，停灵柩于殿内。

Palace of Heavenly Purity (Qianqinggong)
Built in 1420, the double-eaved building rises 24 metres high and is decorated with minute paintings. It is the most important building in the Inner Court. During the Ming and Qing dynasties it served as the living quarters of the emperor, who also attended to state affairs here. The emperor was also laid in state in the palace when he died.

金殿　乾清宫丹陛下左右各有一座文石台，东台上置江山金殿，西台上置社稷金殿。寓意皇帝坐镇江山，一揽天下。

Gilded Pavilion　There is a gilded pavilion on either side of the marble terrace before the Palace of Heavenly Purity. The one on the east is called Jiangshan (country) Pavilion, and the one on the west is called Sheji (government) Pavilion.

乾清宫内景　方形地平床上设金漆雕龙宝座和屏风，其上悬“正大光明”横匾，这是清代自雍正皇帝（1723－1735在位）以后，皇帝为避免皇子间争夺皇位继承权而秘藏立储遗诏之处。

Inside the Palace of Heavenly Purity In the centre of the main hall there is a square platform with a throne and an ornate dragon screen, both of which are gold painted and decorated with delicate carvings. High up in the middle of the hall there is a plaque with an inscription which reads "Be open and above-board". The emperors of the Qing Dynasty after Emperor Yongzheng would write the name of his successor, put the paper in a box and hide the box behind the plaque. The box was opened when the emperor died, thus avoiding the struggle for succeeding to the throne among his sons.

诏书　此诏书为清道光26年（1846）6月26日以满汉两种文字、朱笔书写："皇四子奕詝立为皇太子""皇六子奕訢封为亲王"，并封于储匣内。1850年正月14日道光帝（1821－1850在位）病危，在圆明园召宗人府和军机处诸大臣，公启秘匣，宣布奕詝为皇太了；同日道光驾崩，嗣皇帝继位，年号咸丰，是为清第7代皇帝。此立储御书是保留至今唯一的一份。

Imperial Edict　This Imperial Edict was written in red ink in both Manchu and Chinese on June 26 in the 26th year of the Daoguang Reign of the Qing (1846): "My fourth son Yi Ning is made the crown prince" and "My sixth son Yi Xin is made a prince". The edict was put in a box and the box was sealed off. On the 14th day of the first month in 1850, when Emperor Daoguang was terminally ill, high officials opened the box. On the same day Emperor Daoguang died, and the crown prince became the new emperor entitled Xianfeng. He was the seventh emperor of the Qing Dynasty. This is the only imperial edict that has been kept till today.

乾清宫地平床 为一方形平台，设于正殿中央，平台3级，8扇木雕栏间隔为阶梯，阶梯间置鼎式景泰蓝香炉，平台左右置铜仙鹤，平台正中为宝座和御案。

The Square Platform inside the Palace of Heavenly Purity The square platform is in the centre of the palace and has three stairs. There are eight exquisitely carved wood balustrades along the staircases. Between the balustrades are Ding-style cloisonn é incense burners. Bronze cranes stand on either side of the square platform, and the throne and the imperial desk are put in the centre.

乾清宫宝座 这是整体贴金并镶嵌若干红、绿宝石的金椅，其扶手和靠背均由金龙缠绕而成；座后为金漆屏风，其正中书写着“惟天聪明，惟圣时宪，惟臣钦若，惟民从义”16个金字，概括了皇帝治世之道。

Golden Throne in the Palace of Heavenly Purity The entire throne is gilded and inlaid with ruby and emerald. The handles and back are coiled golden dragons. In the middle of the screen behind the throne are inscribed sixteen golden characters to epitomize the emperor's way of ruling the country.

溥仪　是清代最后一个皇帝，年号宣统，1908年12月2日溥仪在太和殿登基，是年3岁。1911年即宣统3年辛亥革命爆发，次年2月12日清皇室颁发退位诏书，从此结束了中国延续几千年的封建帝制。但是，已下台的末代皇帝仍住紫禁城后廷。1917年6月，北洋军阀张勋率兵入京，7月1日与康有为拥戴溥仪复辟帝制，仅10余天张勋就被另一军阀逐出北京。图为复辟后的溥仪登上乾清宫宝座。

Pu Yi Pu Yi was the last emperor of the Qing Dynasty, entitled Xiantong. On December 2, 1908, when he was three years old, he ascended the throne in the Hall of Supreme Harmony. In the third year of the Xiantong Reign, the 1911 Revolution took place, and on February 12 the following year the Qing Court issued an abdication, thus ending the feudal imperial system that had lasted in China for several thousand years. But the abdicated last emperor still lived in the Forbidden City. In June of 1917, Warlord Zhang Xun headed his troops into Beijing, and together with Kang Youwei, supported Pu Yi to restore monarchy on July 1 that year. But ten days later Warlord Zhang Xun was driven out of Beijing. The picture was taken when Pu Yi ascended the throne in the Palace of Heavenly Purity after the restoration.

交泰殿　其建筑形式如中和殿。“交泰”有“天地相通，协和景运”之意，喻示帝、后和睦、国运昌盛。皇后每逢元旦及生日，在此接受妃嫔、福晋及命妇祝贺；每年仲秋，后妃们在此举行亲蚕仪式。

Hall of Union (Jiaotaidian)　The hall is similar to the Hall of Central Harmony. Its name means "Heaven and earth are united", symbolizing the harmonious relationship between the emperor and the empress. On the New Year Day or birthday of the empress, celebrations were held here. In autumn the empress presided over a ceremony of the silkworm breeding season.

皇帝之宝　交泰殿存有乾隆年间规定的行使各方面权力的宝玺共25方，其中皇帝之宝为檀香木质地，为册立皇后和大典礼专用之玺。此宝是清皇宫若干宝玺中最重要的一方。

Imperial Seals　In the Hall of Union are kept 25 imperials seals of the Qing emperors appraised during the Qianlong Reign. Among them, the one made of sandalwood was used to appoint the empress and hold grand ceremonies. It was the most important one among all the imperial seals in the Qing Court.

乾隆宝玺　乾隆皇帝在位60年，退位后称太上皇，此印即为“太上皇帝”宝玺。

Seal of Emperor Qianlong　Emperor Qianlong reigned for 60 years. After he gave up the throne, he became a retired emperor. This is the seal he used as a retired emperor.

铜壶滴漏　现存于交泰殿，为中国古代计时器，俗称漏壶，有日天壶、夜天壶、平水壶、分水壶和受水壶5部分组成，此壶保存完好，仍可使用，为故宫遗珍。

Water Clock　In the Hall of Union is preserved a clepsydra, a time-piece used in ancient China. It is composed of five bronze vessels, each has a small hole at the bottom. When the uppermost vessel is filled with water, it begins to drip evenly through the holes.

坤宁宫　为重檐庑殿顶，建于1420年，1655年重建，宫室格局仿沈阳清宁宫式样，室内沿山墙为通联大炕，宫室前后装有双菱花窗，窗纸糊在窗外，仍保留着满族风俗。坤宁宫阔9间，正室7间，最西间供贮佛亭，中4间是祭神吃肉场所，东2间为帝后大婚洞房，俗称东暖阁。

Palace of Earthly Tranquillity (Kunninggong)

This palace with a double-eaved hipped roof was built in 1420 and rebuilt in 1655. Inside the palace along the back wall is a broad kang. The front and back windows are decorated with double-diamond designs and papered from the outside in keeping with the Manchu's customs. The Palace of Earthly Tranquillity is nine bays wide. The main hall is seven bays wide. The part at the western end was for keeping the statue of God, the central part was for the emperor to worship God and eat sacrificial meat, and the eastern part was the bridal chamber for the emperor and the empress.

大婚洞房 仍保留着光绪皇帝（1875－1908在位）大婚时的陈设。进入东暖阁，首先看到朱漆影壁，正中有沥粉贴金的大“囍”字，四角饰龙凤相拥的双喜图案，取帝后合卺意，称为“开门见喜”。图为洞房一角。

Bridal Chamber The bridal chamber has preserved the decorations used at the wedding of Emperor Guangxu (reigned from 1875 to 1908). On a red wooden screen wall are the auspicious characters "Double Happiness", and its four corners are decorated with the patterns of a dragon and a phoenix surrounding the characters "Double Happiness", symbolizing the happy marriage of the emperor and the empress. This is called "Doorstep Happiness". In the picture is one corner of the bridal chamber.

龙凤喜床　上铺大红缎绣“囍”字大炕褥，床头置龙凤炕几，床里正中置条桌一张，上放金瓶，内装珠宝、金、银、米、谷等物，称百宝瓶；床楣上挂“日升月恒”匾，喻意帝、后如日初升、月亮上弦。

Dragon-Phoenix Bed　On the bed is a large mattress with "Double Happiness" embroidered on its satin cover. At the head of the bed is a Dragon-Phoenix table, and at the middle on the inside of the bed is a long table with a treasure bottle containing jewelry, gold, silver, rice and millets. Over the front of the bed is a plaque with an inscription, which reads "The sun at dawn and the moon at the first quarter", referring to the emperor and the empress.

百子帐　喜床悬挂特制的大红缎绣龙凤百子图幔帐，百子婴童憨态、活泼可爱，象征皇帝子孙兴旺，后裔昌盛。

Hundred-Baby Drapery　A drapery over the entire bridal bed is made of red satin and embroidered with the design of dragons, phoenixes and a hundred young boys in various postures, symbolizing the fertility of the imperial family.

大婚图　此图为局部，反映的是太和殿前皇帝大婚时的隆重场面。

Grand Wedding　The picture shows the emperor's grand wedding taken place in front of the Hall of Supreme Harmony.

坤宁门雪景　此门设于坤宁宫后，门的东西庑诸房是太监值房，其西为太医值房，出门即为御花园；明代称为“后苑”，此园是中国现存最大、最完整的宫廷花园。

Gate of Earthly Tranquillity in the Snow The gate is located behind the Palace of Earthly Tranquillity. The houses on the eastern side were for eunuchs on duty, and the ones on the western side were for imperial doctors on duty. Behind the gate is the Imperial Garden, which was called "The Back Garden" in the Ming Dynasty. The garden is the best-preserved, largest palace garden extant in China.

千秋亭　建于明代，初为供佛的庙宇，清代用于供奉同治皇帝（1862－1874在位）的牌位；与此亭相对的花园东侧还有一座万春亭，为供奉蜀汉名将关羽（？－公元220）牌位的庙宇。二亭均为上圆下方四出抱厦的重檐亭，造型别致，为园中较具特色的建筑。

Pavilion of a Thousand Autumns Built in the Ming Dynasty, the pavilion first served as a hall for worshipping Buddha, but in the Qing Dynasty it was used to worship the memorial tablet of Emperor Tongzhi (reigned from 1862 to 1874). Opposite to this pavilion in the garden is a similar pavilion called the Pavilion of Ten-Thousand Springs, which was used to worship the memorial tablet of Guan Yu (? - 220 A.D.), a famous general of the state of Shu in the Three Kingdoms period. With a double-eaved round roof, the two pavilions are unique buildings in the Imperial Garden.

香炉　为故宫第一炉，高4米，炉身有6个“二龙戏珠”的火焰喷门，底座铸“三狮戏珠”浮图。它与“北京三绝”之一的雍和宫香炉齐名。

Incense Burner　This bronze incense burner, the largest in the Palace Museum, is four metres high. The six smoke outlets are in the shape of two dragons playing a ball. A relief design on the bottom depicts three lions playing a ball. This bronze incense burner is equal to the one in the Yonghe Palace, which is one of "Beijing's Three Wonders".

金鱼池　澄瑞亭东侧的金鱼池，池中睡莲吐艳、金鱼嬉戏，一静一动，绿肥红瘦，相映成趣。

Goldfish Pond　The pond is located on the eastern side of the Pavilion of Pure Felicity. It is a wonderful sight when water lilies are in blossom and goldfish swim among them.

钦安殿　殿顶为中国古建中罕见的四坡式；殿内供奉玄武大帝和铜制仙官像，是一座道教庙宇。每年正月初一，皇帝拈香拜玄武水神，以避宫中火灾。

Hall of Imperial Peace (Qin'andian) The hall has a uniquely-shaped roof seldom seen in ancient Chinese buildings. Inside it is the statue of Xuanwu King flanked by bronze statues, who was believed to be the Water God. On the first day of the first lunar month every year, the emperor would come to worship the Water God, begging it to prevent the palace buildings from catching fire.

盒飯

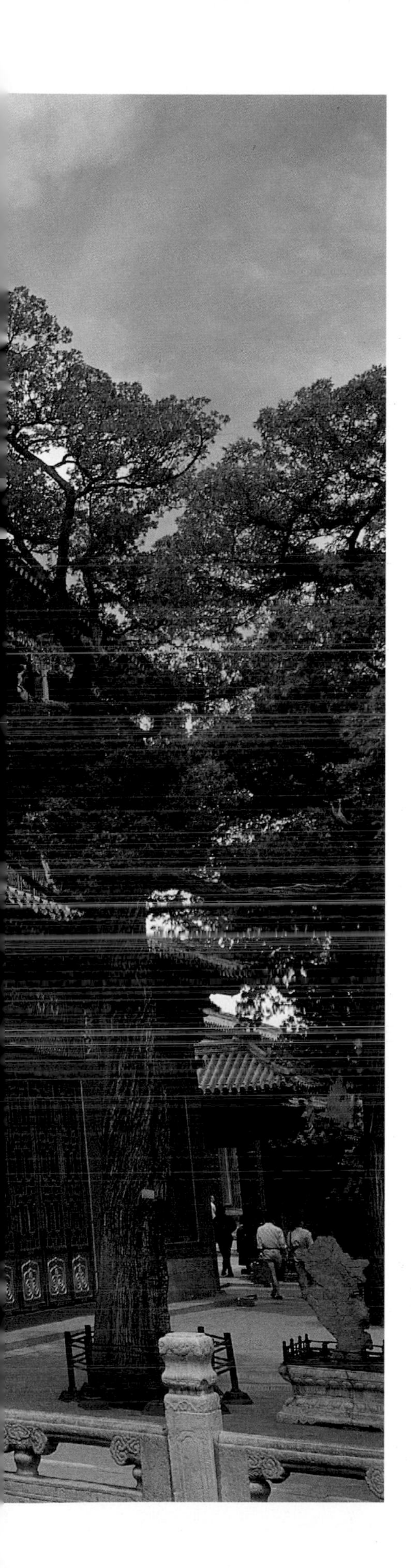

延晖阁　重檐卷棚歇山顶，高15米，宽3间，清代皇帝和大臣常于此赏景吟诗，室内诗联语匾尚存。

Pavilion of Lasting Splendor (Yanhuige)　With a curved-canopy gabled roof, the pavilion is 15 metres high and in three bays. During the Qing Dynasty the emperor and court officials oftcn came here to enjoy the scenery and compose poems. There are still poems and antithetical couplets inside the pavilion today.

东西六宫
Six Eastern Palaces and Six Western Palaces

分列于后三宫的东西两侧，是明清两代妃嫔居所，即民间所说的“三宫六院”、七十二妃嫔、粉黛三千的后宫院，全部为庭院式建筑，方形，深广各50米。每一庭院的主殿座落于主轴线上，东西配殿对称，左右耳房相配，构成前朝后寝的两进格局。东西六宫四面有宫墙环绕，各庭院相对独立，但又互为依存，整体设计严谨有序，建筑规制大体统一，虽有千门万户但又秩序井然。

The Six Eastern Palaces and Six Western Palaces, located on the two sides of the three rear palaces, were the residences of imperial concubines in the Ming and Qing dynasties. Folk people call these buildings "the three palaces and six yards" where 72 imperial concubines and 3,000 beautiful young women lived. With a surrounding wall each palace forms a compound. The main halls stand in the middle and the side-chambers are in the east and west. The hall in the front yard was used for formal audience, and the hall in the back yard served as bed-chamber. The architecture of the 12 palaces are much similar, and they are connected by passageways.

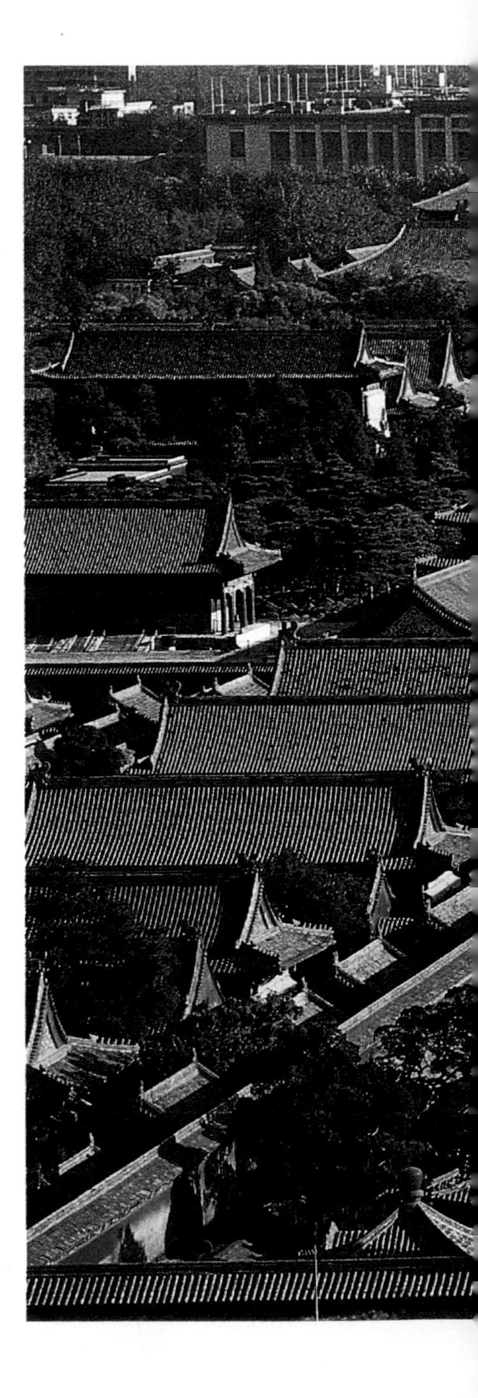

东六宫一瞥　东六宫包括景仁宫、承乾宫、钟粹宫、延禧宫、永和宫和景阳宫。

Bird's-eye view of the Six Eastern Palaces The Six Eastern Palaces include the Palace of Great Benevolence, Palace of Heavenly Inheritance, Palace of Quintessence, Palace of Prolonged Happiness, Palace of Eternal Harmony and Palace of Great Brilliance.

景仁宫　建于明代。清代多位皇后在此住过。清末光绪皇帝宠妃珍妃亦住此宫，珍妃死后，人去楼空。

Palace of Great Benevolence (Jingrengong)　Built in the Ming Dynasty, the palace was the living place of many empresses of the Qing Dynasty. A favourite concubine, Zhenfei, of Emperor Guangxu (1874-1908) once lived here too. After she was murdered by the empress dowager, the palace remained vacant for a long time.

承乾宫　明末崇祯皇帝（1628－1644在位）宠妃田贵妃住此宫，田贵妃文静纤妍，性寡言，多才艺，本为信王朱由校妻，后为崇祯妃。清代顺治皇帝（1644－1661在位）宠妃董鄂氏亦住此宫，董妃21岁死，死后顺治哀极，声言出家当和尚，半年后随妃而去。皇帝为妃而死，恐为极例。

Palace of Heavenly Inheritance (Chengqiangong) Lady Tian, a favourite concubine of Emperor Chongzhen (reigned from 1628 to 1644) of the Ming lived here. A talented and quiet woman, Lady Tian was the wife of Prince Xin, Zhu Youxiao, but later became an imperial concubine. In the Qing Dynasty, a favourite concubine of Emperor Shunzhi (reigned from 1644 to 1661) also lived in this palace.

钟粹宫　明清两代均有皇子住过此宫。皇帝每遇大典时住斋宫，皇后则住钟粹宫。中国末代皇帝溥仪初入宫时，曾居于此。

Palace of Quintessence (Zhongcuigong)　The palace served as the residence of the crown prince during the Ming and Qing dynasties. On the occasion to worship Heaven, the emperor stayed in the Palace of Abstinence and the empress stayed in the Palace of Quintessence. Pu Yi, the last emperor in China, once stayed in this palace.

永和宫 明代为贵妃居所；清代皇帝和多位皇妃住过此宫。

Palace of Eternal Harmony (Yonghegong) This palace was the residence of imperial concubines during the Ming Dynasty, but became a residence of the emperor and many imperial concubines in the Qing.

►

斋宫　是皇帝祭天、祈谷前斋戒、沐浴的寝宫。按典制规定，祭天前3天，皇帝必须到斋宫独宿3昼夜，此间不食荤腥，不饮酒、不娱乐、不近女色、不理刑名，这就是所谓“斋戒”。此宫建于清雍正年间，称“内斋”，天坛斋宫称“外斋”。

Palace of Abstinence (Zhaigong)　The ancient tradition required the emperors of both the Ming and Qing dynasties to worship Heaven and pray for good harvest in the Temple of Heaven on winter solstice. Three days before the event, the emperor had to stay in the Palace of Abstinence, where he was supposed to eat no meat, have no contact with women, drink no wine, have no merry-making and be concerned with no legal matters. This palace was built during the reign of Emperor Yongzheng of the Qing Dynasty.

景阳宫　明代神宗皇帝（1573－1619在位）的孝靖皇后曾居此。1686年重修，后为藏书之所。后殿名为“御书房”，康熙皇帝为皇子时，曾在此读书。

Palace of Great Brilliance (Jingyanggong) Empress Xiaojing of Emperor Shenzong (reigned from 1573 to 1619) of the Ming Dynasty once lived here. The palace was rebuilt in 1686 during the Qing Dynasty. The rear hall served as the Imperial Study. When Emperor Kangxi was crown prince he took his lessons here.

奉先殿　为中国封建社会的五坛八庙之一，类似皇家供奉列祖列宗牌位的太庙。所不同的是，这里不仅供先帝先后灵位，未作过皇帝的先祖牌位亦可在此供奉，以展后辈“孝思之诚”。此殿现为珍宝馆的一部分，内有金、玉、瓷、竹漆器等展品。

Hall of Ancestral Worship (Fengxiandian)　It was one of the Five Imperial Shrines and Eight Temples in ancient China. This hall in the Imperial Palace functioned as the ancestral shrine of the royal family. It is now an exhibition room displaying many art treasures.

大自鸣钟　此钟距今已200多年，仍完好，原置于皇极殿，为乾隆皇帝退位后专用。

Chiming Clock Made in over 200 years ago, this chiming clock is well preserved today. It was originally put in the Hall of Supremacy for the use of Emperor Qianlong after he gave up the throne.

西六宫鸟瞰

Bird's-eye view of the Six Western Palaces

西二长街　为西六宫南北向的第二条长街，街两旁置路灯，灯高2.45米，灯罩为铜质方形重檐攒尖顶，镶玻璃，下部为汉白玉石座。设灯为在夜间巡查关防。

Xi'er Long Road It is the second road of the Six Western Palaces running from south to north, with bronze road lamps on both sides. The road lamps, 2.45 metres high, have a bronze shade with a double-eaved square roof and glass and a white marble stand. They were set there for night patrol.

翊坤宫　西六宫之一，1887年慈禧太后住此宫，并在此受贺50寿辰。翊坤宫东间供慈禧画像。

Palace of Assisting the Empress (Yikungong) One of the Six Western Palaces, it was the place Empress Dowager Cixi lived in 1887 and celebrated her 50th birthday. Inside the palace, on the eastern side is a portrait of Empress Dowager Cixi.

慈禧太后画像　1905年荷兰画家华士·胡博(Hubert VOS)应聘为慈禧太后画像，是年她已七旬，但画面却年轻风韵，显然是画家有意所为。

Portrait of Empress Dowager Cixi　The portrait was painted by the Dutch artist Hubert VOS in 1905 when the empress was seventy years old. But the artist purposely painted her as much younger.

储秀宫　此宫与东六宫的钟粹宫相对称。慈禧太后发迹前曾以贵人身份入住后殿，并在此生下同治皇帝。她50大寿时，在储秀、体和、翊坤宫等处举行盛大庆典，耗资甚巨。民国初年，溥仪的皇后婉容住此宫。

Palace of Gathering Elegance (Chuxiugong) One of the Six Western Palaces, it stands opposite the Palace of Quintessence across the central axis. Empress Dowager Cixi moved to live here after she was promoted to Ladyship and gave birth to the future Emperor Tongzhi. A grand ceremony was held here on her 50th birthday. In the early Republic the dethroned emperor Pu Yi and his wife Wan Rong once lived in this palace.

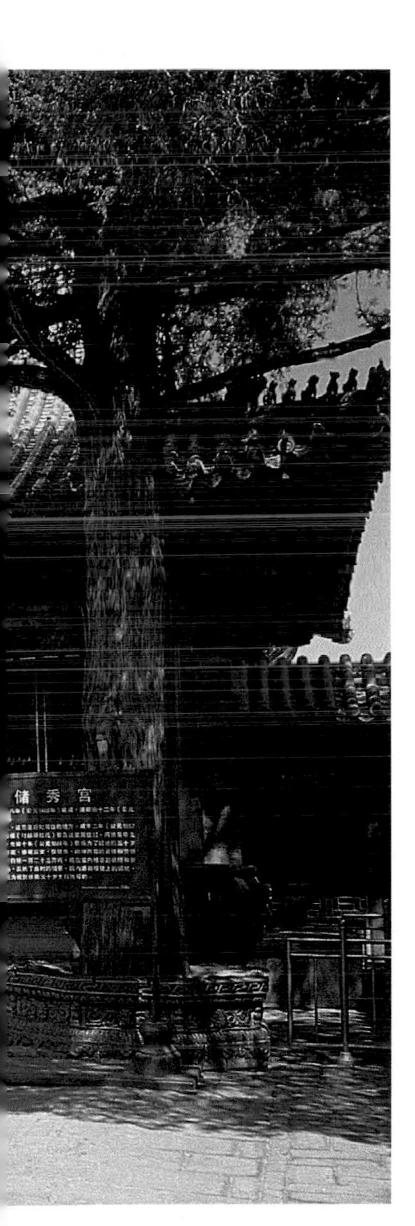

铜龙　龙和凤一样，是中国原始民族信仰的一种图腾，中国历代皇帝皆以真龙自诩，世称“真龙天子”。但把龙设于妃嫔居所储秀宫前，疑是慈禧太后谕制。

Bronze Dragon　Like the phoenix, the dragon was a totem in ancient times. Emperors of the past dynasties regarded themselves as "real dragons" and were called "Real Dragon and Son of Heaven". The bronze dragon in the picture is placed in the Palace of Gathering Elegance. It was believed to be made at the order of Empress Dowager Cixi.

储秀宫正殿　宫内装修精巧华丽，为六宫之冠。正中设宝座，上悬“大圆宝镜”匾，宝座左有雕漆唾盒，右有白玉如意一柄；座前圆几上置青玉万年青盆景，寓意大清帝国一统万年。这里是慈禧太后接受问安之所。

Main Hall of the Palace of Gathering Elegance This palace is the best decorated among the six palaces. At the centre is a throne with a plaque hung above it. On the left of the throne is a carved lacquer spittoon, on the right is a jade object, and in the front, on the round table are placed two pots of evergreen. Empress Dowager Cixi sat on this throne to receive court ministers.

储秀宫东间　室内富丽堂皇，北窗长几上陈设牙雕祝寿龙船和凤船，船长91.5cm，宽35cm，高58cm，其上刻有福、禄、寿三星等42个人物，这是大臣们在慈禧太后生日时献给她的寿礼。

Eastern Part of the Palace of Gathering Elegance Inside the magnificent palace there are two ivory boats, one in the shape of a dragon and the other in the shape of a phoenix. Both are 91.5 cm. long, 35 cm. wide and 58 cm. high. Forty-two immortals are carved on the boats. They were birthday presents of court ministers to Empress Dowager Cixi.

慈禧太后卧床　置于储秀宫西暖阁，床上设檀木葫芦炕罩，其上透雕子孙万代图案。床上铺锦绣缎被，张挂三层苏绣幔帐，皆为五彩绸所做。如此奢华的床上陈设，在宫中仅此而已。

Empress Dowager Cixi's "Dragon Bed" The bed is in the western warm chamber of the Palace of Gathering Elegance. On the bed is a screen of sandalwood carved with many young boys. The quilts, mattresses and three layers of drapery are of colourful silk and satin. This bed is the most extravagantly decorated in the Imperial Palace.

太极殿　中国古人所谓“太极”有万物本源之意，以此作殿名，象征皇族源远流长，洪福齐天。清同治皇帝的瑜妃曾居住此殿。

Hall of Supremacy (Taijidian)　"Supremacy" in ancient China meant the Heavenly Palace and Immortal Land. Lady Yu, a concubine of Emperor Tongzhi, once lived in this hall.

太极殿影壁　故宫东西六宫每组院落大都设影壁，这是明清宫殿建筑定制。影壁多为木制，上饰吉祥图案或吉祥词语，既遮挡正屋视线，又有装饰效果。

Screen Walls　In every compound of the Six Eastern Palaces and Six Western Palaces there is a wooden screen wall inscribed with auspicious words. This is the wooden screen in the compound of the Hall of Supremacy.

太极殿内景　正间设宝座，暖阁为卧室，檀木透雕隔扇作为分割房间的屏障，既有装饰作用，又便于会客和寝卧。

The Interior of the Hall of Supremacy The throne is in the middle, and the bedroom is in the warm chamber, with partition boards carved out of sandalwood standing in between. The carved partition boards serve both as a decoration and a screen.

长春宫　宫名含有春光长驻之意。明清两代多位皇后和妃嫔住过此宫。图为从小戏台看长春宫。戏台是奉慈禧太后谕旨由太极殿后殿和长春门改建的，她50岁生日时，曾在此演戏恭贺。

Palace of Eternal Spring (Changchungong) Several empresses and imperial concubines of the Ming and Qing dynasties lived in this palace. In the picture is the palace viewed from the small open-air theatre, which was built in the compound for the 50th birthday of Empress Dowager Cixi.

长春宫寝宫 陈设色调淡素，大幅工笔淑女图装饰墙面，氛围清新舒适，颇有生活气息。

The Interior of the Palace of Eternal Spring The inside of the palace is furnished in good taste, with large figure paintings on the walls. It is extremely elegant.

雨花阁　从长春宫院落西眺，可见雨花阁宝顶，4条巨龙匍匐在四角攒尖的屋脊上，赫然醒目。此阁为宫内最高佛堂。

Pavilion of Raining Flower (Yuhuage)　Viewed from the compound of the Palace of Eternal Spring, the top of the pavilion comes into sight. The hipped roof is covered with yellow tiles with four galloping dragons on the four ridges. It is the highest building for worshipping Buddha in the Imperial Palace.

养心殿　位于西六宫南面，占地5000多平方米，四周有高大红墙环绕，自成一院。慈禧太后揽权期间，所谓"垂帘听政"就发生在这里。

Hall of Mental Cultivation (Yangxindian) Located on the southern side of the Six Western Palaces, the hall covers an area of over 5,000 square metres with high red walls surrounding it. It has an independent compound. Empress Dowager Cixi ruled China behind the curtain in this hall.

藻井　大堂天花板正中是浑金蟠龙藻井，井内金龙盘卧，口衔巨形轩辕球，以示中国皇帝皆为轩辕氏皇帝正统继承者。

Caisson Ceiling　The gilded caisson ceiling is decorated with a dragon pattern. Hanging underneath are glass balls called "Mirrors of the Yellow Emperor" which represent orthodox succession.

养心殿大堂　堂内设公案、宝座，其后正中悬雍正皇帝御题的"中正仁和"匾。这里是清代皇帝召见大臣、引见官员的地方。典制规定，凡官员升迁、补缺、调动，或任期届满，均须在此跪见皇帝，奏报履历，听其训喻。

Inside the Hall of Mental Cultivation　Inside the hall there are imperial desk and throne. In the centre of the hall hangs a horizontal board bearing the Chinese characters "Justice and Benevolence" in Emperor Yongzheng's handwriting. This is where the emperor gave audience to court officials.

中正仁和

养心殿东暖阁　这里是“辛酉政变”后慈禧、慈安两太后“垂帘听政”处。黄色纱帘前后设两个宝座，小皇帝坐前面，仅作摆设，一切军政大事均由帘后太后决定。6岁的同治皇帝和4岁的光绪皇帝先后在此充当傀儡。

East Warm Chamber of the Hall of Mental Cultivation　This is the place Empress Dowagers Cixi and Ci'an took over the power and began to "hold court behind curtain" after the 1861 Coup. There was a yellow gauze curtain between the two thrones. The child emperor was seated on the throne in front, while the two empress dowagers were seated on the large throne behind. Both the six-year-old child emperor Tongzhi and the four-year-old child emperor Guangxu were seated on the smaller throne as puppets.

三希堂　为养心殿西暖阁仅8平方米的一间小屋，乾隆皇帝将中国历史上著名的书法家王羲之（公元303－361）的《快雪时晴帖》、王献之（公元344－386）的《中秋帖》和王珣（公元350－401）的《伯远帖》等3件希世珍宝藏于此，故名“三希堂”。

Room of Three Rarities (Sanxitang) It is a 8-square-metre room in the West Warm Chamber of the Hall of Mental Cultivation. Emperor Qianlong of the Qing kept three samples of calligraphy by Wang Xizhi (303-361), Wang Xianzhi (344-386) and Wang Xun (350-401), famous calligraphers of the Jin Dynasty, in this room. Hence the name of the room.

皇帝寝宫　图为寝宫外间，隔扇内为皇帝卧室。清代自雍正皇帝以后，历代皇帝均居于此。室内“天行健”、“自强不息”匾均为光绪皇帝手笔。

Bedroom of the Emperor　The bedroom behind the screen was for all the Qing emperors after Yongzheng. The two inscriptions on the horizontal boards "Heaven produces health" and "Constantly strive to become stronger" were in Emperor Guangxu's handwriting.

卧床　皇帝寝宫设两张床，东间床是皇后侍寝时住的，床前罩上悬“又日新”匾为慈禧太后所书，其意为保持德性，日贤于一日。

Beds in the Emperor's Bedroom　There were two beds in the emperor's bedroom. The one in the picture was for the empress. The inscription above it "Forge ahead daily" was in the handwriting of Empress Dowager Cixi, meaning to retain virtue and get perfect everyday.

体顺堂　位于养心殿后东侧。凡皇帝大婚后，帝、后在坤宁宫仅住两天，第三天皇帝移住养心殿，皇后住体顺堂。体顺堂的东围房是应召侍寝妃嫔的临时住所。

Hall of Displaying Obedience (Tishuntang) Located on the eastern side of the Hall of Mental Cultivation, this hall was for the empress. After wedding and living with the empress for two days in the Palace of Earthly Tranquillity, the emperor moved to live in the Hall of Mental Cultivation, while the empress moved to live in the Hall of Displaying Obedience. The surrounding halls on the eastern side were for imperial concubines.

外 东 宫
Outer Eastern Palaces

是乾隆皇帝为自己做满60年皇帝退位后的养怡之所，1796年，乾隆皇帝85岁，决定把皇位“内禅”给儿子颙琰，自称太上皇，外东宫因此也叫太上皇宫殿。

外东宫占地46000平方米，也分前朝、后廷两部分，前朝以皇极殿、宁寿宫为主，是太上皇训政和接受朝贺之处；后廷以养性殿、乐寿堂为主，为太上皇寝宫，其东有畅音阁和阅是楼等燕乐建筑，西有宁寿花园，俨然又一座皇宫。

外东宫建筑群，除体量不如大内正衙外，规制甚高，殿廷辉煌，装饰华贵，各种稀世珍宝，璀璨夺目。为展现皇家珍宝的奇妙，外东宫现已辟为珍宝馆。

In 1796 the 85-year-old Qianlong, after being emperor for 60 years, decided to give the throne to his son and become a retired emperor himself. The Outer Eastern Palaces of 46,000 square metres were specially built for him. This group of buildings is independent of the other parts of the Imperial Palace; however the general plan is made exactly after that on the central axis, i.e. three big halls in the Outer Court and three palaces in the Inner Court. The Outer Court in the south was where the retired Emperor Qianlong received festive greetings from high-ranking officials, whereas the Inner Court in the north served as the residence for him and his empress. Today, the Outer Eastern Palaces are made the museum of jewelry.

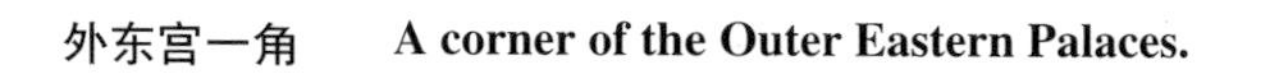
外东宫一角　**A corner of the Outer Eastern Palaces.**

九龙壁　位于皇极门前，为清代3座九龙壁之一。壁高3.5米，长29.4米，由270块彩色琉璃件镶嵌而成；壁面9条彩龙飞腾嬉戏于海涛云雾之中，呼之欲出。

Nine-Dragon Screen　Three Nine-Dragon Screens of the Qing Dynasty have been left in China. The one in the Outer Eastern Palaces is 3.5 metres high, 29.4 metres long and built with 270 glazed multicolored tiles. Nine dragons romp in the sea against a background of waves and clouds.

宁寿门 门为5楹，垂脊歇山式庑殿顶，一对鎏金铜狮镇守门前左右，两侧为琉璃“八字”影壁，建筑规制甚高，其作用如同前朝太和门。

Gate of Tranquil Longevity (Ningshoumen) The gate is much like a palace hall with a single-eaved gabled roof of yellow glazed tiles. Two gilded bronze lions stand on either side. The wall spreading from the gate is covered with glazed tiles.

铜狮　置于宁寿门前。铜狮通体贴金，铸造精美，形象生动。

Bronze Lion　Two gilded bronze lions stand on either side of the Gate of Tranquil Longevity. They look very lifelike.

皇极殿　大殿居中向阳，为太上皇临朝正殿。它重檐庑殿顶，青白石须弥座，丹楹锁窗，金琢墨彩画，一如大内正衙太和殿规制。此殿现为珍宝馆，内藏明清两代皇室珍宝。

Hall of Imperial Supremacy (Huangjidian) It is the main hall of the Palace of Tranquil Longevity built for holding official ceremonies after Emperor Gianlong retired. The magnificent structure has a roof with double eaves, white stone foundation and painted beams. The entire building was modelled after the Hall of Supreme Harmony. Now it is an exhibition room for the treasures of the Ming and Qing dynasties.

皇极殿顶　正中为金龙藻井，天花板沥粉贴金，遍绘彩画。此种彩画金、红、青、绿相间，图案以龙凤为主，称为“和玺彩画”，为皇家专用。

Ceiling of the Hall of Imperial Supremacy　The hall has a gilded caisson ceiling decorated with a dragon-phoenix pattern and beautifully painted in different colours. This decoration is called "hexi painting" specially used in the buildings of the royal family.

乾隆龙袍 是乾隆皇帝在朝会、受贺及重大典礼时穿的朝服，其上绣金丝团龙、行龙共31条，间以日、月、星辰等12章纹饰，可谓花团锦簇，奢华异常。

Emperor Qianlong's Robe Emperor Qianlong wore the robe when he gave audience to court officials or attended grand ceremonies. The robe is embroidered in gold thread with 31 coiling or galloping dragons and 12 patterns of the sun, moon, star and other auspicious objects.

皇后朝褂 实为里袍外褂，褂无袖，形似长马甲，前后各绣立龙两条，下摆精做4层花纹，金龙和万福万寿相间，并有云水纹，是皇后大典时穿的朝服。

Long Gown of the Empress The empress wore this long gown to attend grand ceremonies. It has a long garment inside and a sleeveless gown outside. In the front and back of the gown are embroidered two dragons, and on the lower hem of the gown are four layers of patterns of the dragon, clouds, waves, etc.

金佛塔 乾隆年间制造，是信奉喇嘛教的帝、后拜佛时用的。塔高132cm，用黄金85公斤，大小珍珠千余颗，各种宝石300多块。

Gold Buddhist Pagoda The pagoda was made in the Qianlong Reign of the Qing Dynasty for the emperor and empress to worship Buddha. It is 132 cm. high, made of 85 kilogramme gold, over 1,000 pearls and 300 gems of various kinds.

宁寿宫　制如坤宁宫。东间为卧室，西间是祭神之所。慈禧太后每年腊月和正月在此居住。

Palace of Tranquil Longevity (Ningshougong) The building was modelled after the Palace of Earthly Tranquillity. The east anteroom was the bedroom and the west anteroom served as a shrine where there was a huge wooden coach and sacrificial objects. Empress Dowager Cixi stayed here in the last month of the lunar year and the beginning of a new year.

象牙席 长216cm，宽139cm。制做此席须精选象牙，将其特殊处理后，劈成厚0.1cm、宽0.3cm的薄条编成席；费工费料，甚为艰难。清雍正年间曾制做5件，现存3件。

Ivory Mat It is 216 cm. by 139 cm. and woven of ivory filaments less than 0.3 cm. wide and 0.1 cm. thick. Five ivory mats were made during the Yongzhen Reign of the Qing Dynasty. Three have remained.

青花釉盖罐　中国烧制磁器源远流长，至宋（960－1279）、元（1206－1368）臻于精绝。此件作品以青花为主调，以剔花为特色，十分精细美丽。罐高41cm，口径15.5cm，底径18.5cm。

Blue and White Glazed Porcelain Jar Porcelain making started very early in China, and its craftsmanship became perfect in the Song Dynasty (960-1279) and the Yuan Dynasty (1206-1368). The exquisitely made porcelain jar in the picture is 41 cm. high with its mouth at a diameter of 15.5 cm. and its bottom at a diameter of 18.5 cm.

青玉云纹灯 为战国（前475－前221）遗珍，灯的上盘边沿和柱身阴刻美丽花纹；圆形台座凸雕云朵，造型生动，疑为王公专用。灯高12.8cm，盘径10.2cm，台座径5.9cm。

Jade Lamp with Cloud Design This lamp was handed down from the Warring States period (475-221 B. C.). The edge and the post of the lamp are carved in intaglio with beautiful designs, and the round stand of the lamp is carved in relief with cloud design. The lamp is 12.8 cm. high, with the oil holder at a diameter of 12.8 cm. and lamp stand at a diameter of 5.9 cm.

硝子莲花钵 乾隆年间制造，玉质，钵体晶莹剔透，雕花逼真，极珍贵。钵高12.4cm，口径16.3cm。

Bowl with Lotus Flower Design This bowl, made out of jade in the Qianlong Reign of the Qing Dynasty, is crystal and with beautiful carvings. It is 12.4 cm. high, with a mouth at a diameter of 16.3 cm.

景泰蓝兽耳环尊　景泰蓝为中国特种工艺品之一，器物以紫铜作胎，再把铜丝绕成各种花纹焊在胎上，填上珐琅彩釉，烧制而成。明代景泰年间（1450－1456）在北京开始大量烧制，工艺也趋完善，又因彩釉多为蓝色，所以叫景泰蓝。此尊高约1米，口径36.2cm。

Cloisonné Jar with Animal-Shaped Handles Cloisonné is one of the arts and crafts produced in China, and cloisonné jars are made of bronze with decorations glazed with enamel. They first appeared in the Jingtai Period of the Ming Dynasty (1450-1456). The jar in the picture is one metre high, with its mouth at a diameter of 36.2 cm.

水晶觥　"觥"是中国古代一种酒器，用类似牛角制作的觥叫兕觥。此件水晶觥为清代遗物，系仿古代酒器制成。觥高23.2cm，口径12cm。

Crystal *Gong* *Gong* was an ancient wine vessel made of horn. This crystal *gong* of the Qing Dynasty is an imitation of the ancient wine vessel. It is 23.2 cm. high, and the diameter of its mouth is 12 cm.

天球仪　乾隆年间制造，以黄金做球体，用珍珠镶嵌成星星，以缠绕的金龙做支架，设计巧妙，制作精良，既有观察天象的实用性，又具有工艺品的欣赏性。球高82cm，重6.071公斤。

Celestial Globe　Made in the Qianlong Reign of the Qing Dynasty, this celestial globe has a globe made out of gold and stars inlaid with pearls and a support surrounded by coiling gold dragons. In ingenious design, it can be used as an observing tool and an ornament. It is 82 cm. high, weighing 6.071 kilograms.

日晷　设于养性殿前。日晷是中国古代利用日影测定时间的仪器。故宫的日晷分别安放于太和殿、午门、乾清宫和养性殿前，既为计时，也有皇帝一统授时之意。

Sundial In ancient times people used a sundial to show the time of the day from the shadow cast by an upright pin on a dial. Sundials were placed at the Hall of Supreme Harmony, Meridian Gate, Palace of Heavenly Purity and Hall of Character Cultivation.

养性门 位于宁寿宫后，实为外东宫内廷正门，门东侧有畅音阁戏楼，西有宁寿宫花园，构成了太上皇的小内廷。

Gate of Character Cultivation (Yangxingmen) Located behind the Palace of Tranquil Longevity, the gate is the main entrance to the Inner Court of the Outer Eastern Palaces. On the east of the gate is the Pavilion of Fluent Music and on the east is a garden.

养性殿寝宫 殿名有涵养天性之意，这里是太上皇的寝宫，制同大内养心殿，实际上乾隆退位后并未住过，仅于1782年在此赐宴王公大臣、蒙古王公、贝勒等；慈禧太后住乐寿堂时，在此用膳；1903年各国使节夫人在此觐见光绪皇帝和慈禧太后。图为寝宫东暖阁。

East Warm Chamber of the Hall of Character Cultivation The chamber was for Emperor Qianlong after he retired, but he never lived in it. He only gave a banquet to princes and court officials here in 1782. Later it became a place Empress Dowager Cixi came to dine. In 1903 the wives of diplomatic envoys to China came here to present themselves before Emperor Guangxu and Empress Dowager Cixi.

御用餐具　质地为金、银、瓷，多为乾隆年间制作；唯乾隆皇帝使用的瓷碗是康熙年间（1662－1722）制作的。

Imperial Tableware　Most of these gold, silver and porcelain dinner sets were made in the Qianlong Reign. But the porcelain bowls Emperor Qianlong used were made in the Kangxi Reign (1662-1722).

畅音阁　为清代三大戏楼之一，高20.71米，分上中下三层。下层天花板中心有天井与上层串通，二层戏台设绞车，可巧设机关布景，上天入地，变幻无穷。

Pavilion of Fluent Music (Changyinge)　One of three most famous theatres in the Qing Dynasty, the structure, 20.71 metres high, has three stories. The lower floor has openings in the ceiling so actors could come down from the second floor through them. A capstan was installed under every opening to lift the actors or the setting up to the first floor.

乐寿堂　单檐垂脊，9开间。1894年慈禧太后移居此殿，并在此度过60大寿。1900年八国联军侵入北京，慈禧挟持光绪皇帝就是从这里逃往西安的。

Hall of Happy Longevity (Leshoutang) The hall has a single-eaved roof and nine bays. In 1894 Empress Dowager Cixi moved to live here and celebrated her 60th birthday. In 1900 Empress Dowager Cixi and Emperor Guangxu fled from here for Xi'an when the Eight-Power Allied Forces invaded Beijing.

珍妃井　珍妃为光绪皇帝宠妃，因支持皇帝新政被打入冷宫。1900年八国联军攻入北京，慈禧太后出逃前，令太监将其推入井中溺死，年仅25岁。此井因此得名。

Zhenfei's Well Zhenfei was Emperor Guangxu's favourite concubine, but she was on bad terms with Empress Dowager Cixi for she supported the 1898 Reform Movement. In 1900 the Eight-Power Allied Forces invaded Beijing. Before her fleeing, Empress Dowager Cixi ordered an eunuch to push Zhenfei into the well and she was drowned. Then she was only 25 years old.

大玉山 陈设在乐寿堂后，乾隆皇帝为显示自己法先王圣绩之隆，将大禹治水故事刻于巨玉之上。玉山通高2.24米，宽0.96米，重5吨，是中国现存最大的玉器。

Huge Jade Carving This jade carving is placed at the rear of the Hall of Happy Longevity. Emperor Qianlong ordered to have the story "Dayu Harnessing Floods" carved on the jade in order to show his own achievements. The largest piece of jade carving in China today, it is 2.24 metres high and 0.96 metre wide and weighs 5 tons.

角楼　故宫城墙四隅各设角楼一座，它们均为6个歇山顶组合而成的奇特整体。角楼三层屋檐设计有28个翼角，72条屋脊，造型精巧玲珑，堪称中国古建一绝。

Corner Tower　At each of the four corners of the Imperial Palace stands a unique tower, each with six hipped and gabled roofs. The three-tiered eaves sloping into 28 upturned curves, and together with 72 ridges, add much grace to the structure.

神武门 为故宫北门，高31米。皇后、妃嫔们前往蚕坛举行亲蚕仪式出入此门。

Gate of Divine Prowess (Shenwumen)
The north gate of the Imperial Palace is 31 metres high. The empress and imperial concubines left the palace through this gate to attend the ceremony of starting silkworm breeding season.

东华门　为故宫东门，高33米。文武百官上朝或退值出入东西华门。皇帝驾崩，灵柩由东华门出，故称“鬼门”，因之门钉亦用阴数（偶数），计8行9列72个，以表生死有别。

East Flowery Gate (Donghuamen) It is the east gate of the Imperial Palace. The gate tower is 33 metres high. When officials went to court or came back from it, they always passed through this gate or the West Flowery Gate. In the Qing Dynasty, when the emperor died, his coffin was carried out of the palace through this gate, thus its nickname "the Gate of Ghost". Its 72 door knobs are even in number, because people believed that even numbers and the dead belonged to the same *yin*.

角楼夜景 The corner tower at night

编　　辑 宇　辰
翻　　译 振　儒
责任编辑 恩　博
摄　　影 罗文法　宇　辰
高明义　张肇基
刘思功　孙树明
蔡　荣　胡　锤
姜景余　严向群

Editors: Yuchen Enbo
Translated by: Zhenru
Photos by : Luo Wenfa, Yuchen,
Gao Mingyi, Zhang Zhaoji,
Liu Sigong, Sun Shuming,
Cairong, Huchui,
Jiang Jingyu and Yan Xiangqun

北京皇宫·紫禁城

宇辰　编
振儒　译
*
人民中国出版社出版
北京博诚印刷厂印制
2000年（16开）第一版第一次印刷
ISBN 7 - 80065 - 693 - 4 / J.112 (外)
05000

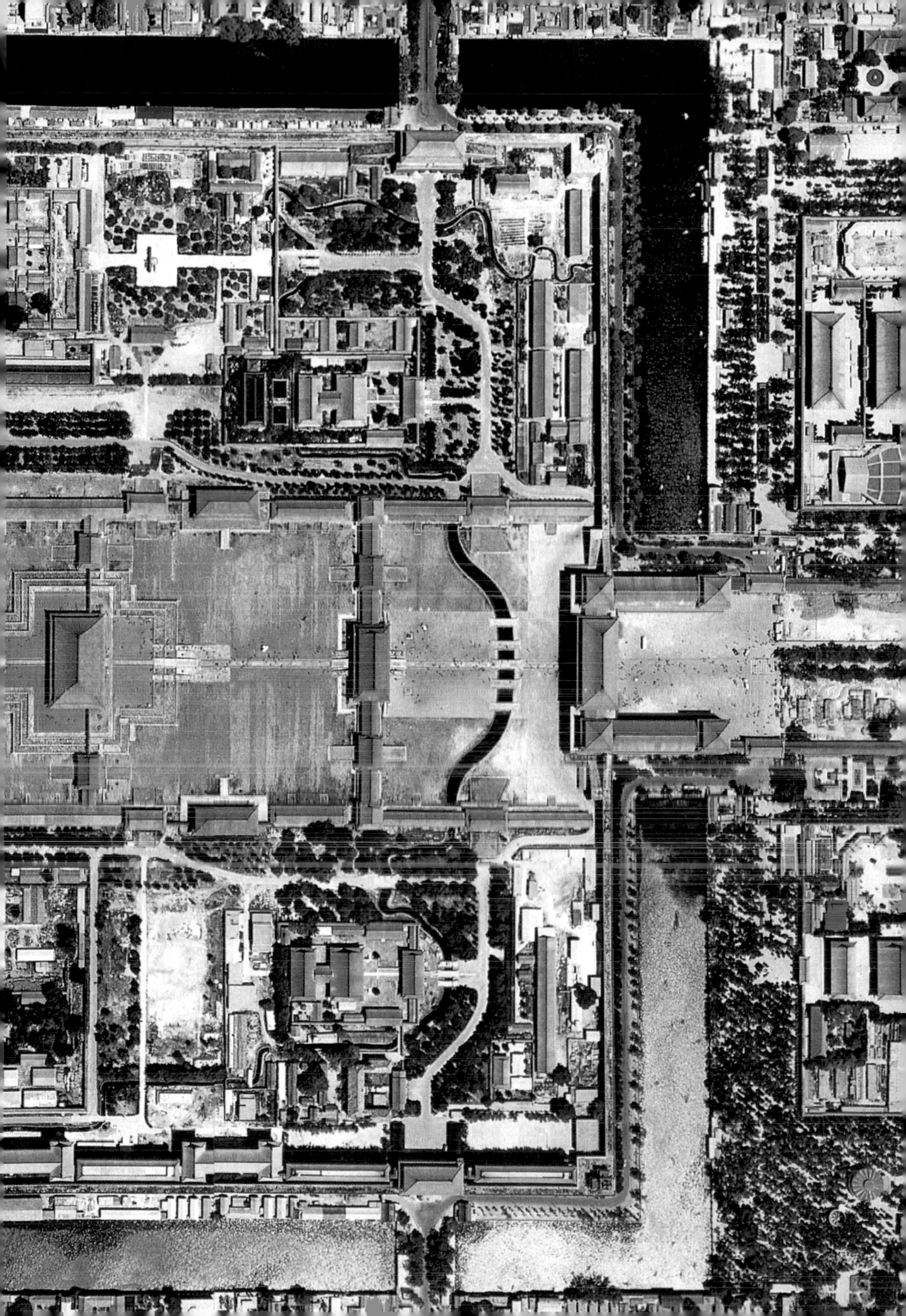